# CONTENTS

Associated publications referred to in the Guidance Notes

ICE Conditions of Contract – Measurement Version 7th Edition

ICE Arbitration Procedure 1997
ICE Arbitration Procedure (Scotland) (1983)
ICE Conciliation Procedure 1999
ICE Adjudication Procedure 1997

Other ICE Conditions of Contract publications

ICE Design and Construct Conditions of Contract
Guidance Notes to the ICE Design and Construct Conditions of Contract
ICE Conditions of Contract Minor Works 2nd Edition (including Guidance Notes)

# INTRODUCTION

Standard agreed forms of conditions of contract (referred to as the ICE Conditions of Contract) for use in connection with works of civil engineering construction have been published since December 1945.

After the publication in June 1973 of the Fifth Edition of the ICE Conditions of Contract a permanent joint committee - the Conditions of Contract Standing Joint Committee (CCSJC) - was set up to keep the use of standard forms of contract under review, to consider any suggestions for amendment and also to undertake the drafting of new standard forms.

The composition of the CCSJC is as follows:

> An independent chairman appointed by the ICE.
> Three members appointed by the ACE to represent Consultants.
> Three members appointed by the CECA to represent Contractors.
> Three members appointed by the ICE on the advice of client bodies to represent Clients.
> One co-opted member (a Fellow or Member of the ICE with an academic or legal background) appointed by the ICE.

The terms of reference of the CCSJC exclude the provision of any legal interpretation.

These Guidance Notes have been prepared by the CCSJC specifically to assist users of the ICE Conditions of Contract in the preparation of contract documents and the carrying out of the contract Works. They do not purport to provide legal interpretation but do represent the unanimous view of the CCSJC on what constitutes good practice in the conduct of civil engineering projects.

Like all previous editions of the ICE Conditions of Contract, the Seventh Edition is based on the traditional pattern of Engineer-designed, Contractor-built Works with valuation by admeasurement. The traditional role of the Engineer in advising his client, designing the Works, supervising construction, certifying payment and deciding what are now called matters of dissatisfaction is fully maintained.

The Contract is drafted bearing in mind the benefits of team working and current procurement initiatives. If its procedures are followed the parties to the Contract will be provided with an "early warning" of circumstances that may give rise to additional costs or delay in a stage or completion of the Contract

To enable the minimisation of additional cost and/or delay as well as potential for dispute all possible steps should be taken to avoid changes to pre-planned Works information. Design work should be completed before tender information is sent out and then not be subject to change. Changes in requirements after contracts have been let will normally lead to substantial increases in cost and undermine the principle of mutual co-operation.

The Contract is also drafted with the intention of minimising the incidence of potential disputes and resolving those that may arise in a speedy and non-confrontational manner. The Contract provides the choice of conciliation, adjudication and arbitration to facilitate the resolution of disputes.

The Housing Grants, Construction and Regeneration Act 1996 came into force on 1 May 1998 for construction contracts as defined in the Act. The Contract is drafted to comply with this legislation with the intention that the Statutory "Scheme for Construction Contracts" should not apply (see in particular Clauses 60 and 66). Clause 67 deals with the application of the legislation to Scotland and the Construction Contracts (Northern Ireland) Order in Northern Ireland.

Compared with previous editions, several substantial changes and a number of minor ones have been made and a certain amount of editing has been carried out to improve the clarity of the document.

It should be noted that these Guidance Notes should not and do not form part of the Contract.

## CONTRACT DOCUMENTS

When Clauses 1 to 72 of the ICE Conditions of Contract are incorporated in a Contract it is recommended that they are incorporated unaltered because they are closely interrelated and any changes made in some may have unforeseen effects on others.

If it is necessary on a particular Contract to make any special contractual arrangements these should be effected by the addition of special conditions in accordance with Clause 72 of the ICE Conditions of Contract. Special conditions should be kept to the minimum necessary to cover the special circumstances of the particular project. The practice of including as special conditions matters which are more appropriate to the Specification should be avoided.

This procedure assists comprehension of the documents, particularly at the tender stage, because it obviates the need for tenderers to scrutinize the standard conditions to check for possible amendments or additions.

## TENDER DOCUMENTATION AND PROCEDURES

It is recommended that the procedures set out in the publication "Tendering for Civil Engineering Contracts" be followed.

It is important for Employers to be fully aware of the recommendations made in respect of tendering procedures, and for them to avoid putting undue pressure on Engineers to send out invitations to tender before the design and preparation of the Drawings and other contract documents have been completed. Employers should also allow adequate time for the preparation of tenders.

## MATTERS FOR THE EMPLOYER TO DECIDE DURING THE PREPARATION OF THE TENDER DOCUMENTS

Under the ICE Conditions of Contract the Employer has to appoint an Engineer (who may be a person, firm or company) to design the Works, prepare the Contract documents and supervise the construction of the Works as well as generally administering the contract. If the Engineer so appointed is not a single named Chartered Engineer the Engineer has a duty, after the award of the Contract, to notify to the Contractor in writing the name of a Chartered Engineer who will act on his behalf and assume the full responsibilities of the Engineer under the Contract.

One of the first appointments an Employer has to make is that of the Planning Supervisor under the Construction (Design and Management) Regulations 1994 (more commonly known as the CDM Regulations) (Clause 71(1)(b)). Under these Regulations the Planning Supervisor is required, in the first instance, to manage the preparation of the Health and Safety Plan. Other duties are referred to in Clause 71 of these Notes, however, as the Notes are not exhaustive, the Regulations should be studied in detail.

During the preparation of the tender documents the Employer, generally in consultation with or with advice from the Engineer, must decide

(a)    the duration of the Defects Correction Period (Clause 1(1)(s) and Part I of the Appendix to the Form of Tender)

(b)    the number and type of Drawings to be provided to the Contractor (Clause 6(1)(b))

(c)    which parts of the Permanent Works, if any, are to be designed by the Contractor (Clause 7(6))

(d)    whether or not a formal Contract Agreement will be required from the successful Contractor (Clause 9)

(e)    whether a performance bond will be required from the successful Contractor, and if so its amount (Clause 10)

(f)    what information he has relevant to the Works and which is to be passed to the Engineer so that details can be included in the documentation prepared for the Contract. (In this connection it would be advisable for the Employer to note carefully the contents of the Guidance Note for Clause 11)

(g)    the minimum level of third party insurance to be called for (Clause 23(3))

(h)    the commencement date for the Contract (Clause 41(1)) if this is to be pre-set

(i)    what restrictions, if any, apply to the availability of any part or parts of the Site and/or the access to the Site (Clause 42(1))

(j)    whether provision should be included for Sectional completion (Clause 43)

(k)      the time that should be allowed for completion of the Works or (if appropriate) any Section of the Works (Clause 43)*

(l)      the level of, and any limit to, any liquidated damages to be levied for any delay in substantial completion of the Works or (if appropriate) each Section of the Works (Clause 47)

(m)      whether provision should be made for payment for materials not on Site under the vesting procedure (Clause 54(4))*

(n)      what work, if any, should be carried out by Nominated Sub-contractors (Clause 59) and whether they are required to design the same (Clause 58(3))

(o)      the percentage of their value to be paid for materials on site or vested in the Employer (Clause 60(2)(b))

(p)      the minimum amount of an interim certificate to be paid (Clause 60(3))

(q)      the rate and limit of retention money to be held (Clause 60(5))

(r)      the bank whose base lending rate is to be used in calculating any interest due on a late payment (Clause 60(7))

(s)      whether to appoint a named Adjudicator to act under the provisions of Clause 66(4)

(t)      on the arrangements for the Principal Contractor to be appointed under the Construction (Design and Management) Regulations 1994 (Clause 71(1)(b))

(u)      the extent to which the Health and Safety plan for the Works required under the Construction (Design and Management) Regulations 1994 (Clause 71(1)(c)) and the Health and Safety Files in respect of each of the structures included in the Works need to be prepared and to be available for issue to or inspection by tenderers

(v)      whether to include a Contract Price Fluctuation Clause.

Any requirements where the Employer's approval has to be obtained before the Engineer can act as required under the Contract must be listed in the Appendix to the Form of Tender (see Clause 2(1)(b)).

* If so decided by the Employer these matters may be left for the Contractor to complete when tendering.

# NOTES ON SPECIFIC CLAUSES

**Clause 1(1)(a):**
**Employer**

The Employer has a number of duties to perform under the Contract.

If a Contract Agreement (Clause 9) is required by the Employer he is responsible for its preparation. The Employer also has responsibility for approving the Contractor's performance security (Clause 10(1)). For his own protection he should also check the terms and coverage of the Contractor's insurance policies and verify that premiums have been paid (Clauses 25(1) and (3)).

The Employer is responsible for ensuring that the Contractor will be given possession of and access to the Site to enable him to commence and proceed with the Works. Any restrictions must be set out in the contract documents. The Employer is also responsible for ensuring that payments are made to the Contractor by the final date for payment following certification by the Engineer.

The Employer has the power, in certain circumstances, to terminate the employment of the Contractor.

**Clause 2:**
**Duties and authority of**
**Engineer**

The Engineer is appointed by the Employer to supervise the Contract and to that end the Engineer has conferred on him by both Parties the powers and duties vested in him under the Contract.

It is in the interests of both the Employer and the Contractor that any queries or problems that arise during construction should be resolved expeditiously. To this end the Contract requires that the Engineer's function shall be exercised by a single named Chartered Engineer even though the appointed Engineer may have been a person, firm or company.

If Clause 2(2)(a) applies and/or Clause 2(2)(b) could apply and the Employer decides that it will be necessary for a person who is not a Chartered Engineer to be appointed to assume the full responsibilities of the Engineer under the Contract this must be drawn to the attention of Contractors tendering when tenders are invited.

Good practice dictates that the Engineer, when carrying out his functions under the ICE Conditions of Contract, should keep the Employer informed of progress, performance, variations and all other relevant matters.

*Engineer's independence and impartiality*

The Engineer acts as the agent of the Employer to supervise the construction of the Works and to satisfy himself that the Works are being constructed in accordance with the Contract. Of no less importance are those functions which require the Engineer to make decisions regarding any changes to the Works that need to be made in the course of construction or which arise from the allocation of risks. In all aspects of his duties under the Contract both the Engineer and the Engineer's Representative are required by Clause 2(7) to act in accordance with the terms of the Contract, impartially, towards both parties to the Contract, having regard to all the circumstances.

The Engineer has the duty to exercise his professional judgement, honestly and impartially to decide such matters as unforeseen conditions (Clause 12), extensions of time (Clause 44), the valuation of variations to the Works (Clause 52) and to formally decide any issues where either the Employer or Contractor are dissatisfied (Clause 66).

Provision is made in the ICE Conditions of Contract for the Employer to stipulate that his approval must be obtained before the Engineer exercises his authority on specific matters. The particular matters on which the Engineer can only so act after receipt of approval from the Employer must be clearly set out in the Appendix to the Form of Tender (Clause 2(1)(b)) so that the Contractor is aware of the restrictions imposed at the time of tender.

It follows that if the Employer has placed restrictions on the powers of the Engineer before the Contract is made that prevent the Engineer acting without prior approval, the responsibility for acting within the terms of the Contract is assumed by the Employer. Any action or any failure to act on his part which is not within the terms of the Contract may render him liable for damages.

**Clause 3(2): Rights of Third Parties**

By this Clause the acquisition of rights by third parties is excluded.

**Clause 4: Sub-contracting**

Clause 4 recognises the practice in the construction industry of the use of sub-contractors and self-employed labour. In general the Contractor should be free to choose his own sub-contractors.

There are two aspects to Clause 4(2). The first allows the Employer, at the tender stage, to advise the Contractor via the Appendix to the Form of Tender of those aspects of the work which the Contractor must not sub-contract to others without the specific authority of the Engineer.

The second aspect requires the Contractor to advise the Engineer of the name and address of a proposed sub-contractor at least 14 days in advance of that sub-contractor's entry on to the Site. The Contractor should take care not to create a binding obligation to his sub-contractor until he is sure the Engineer will not object.

Any objections to a specific sub-contractor must be made within 7 days of receiving the notification from the Contractor. It is essential that the Engineer not only gives his reasons for objection but also that these must be in writing. The reasons must be good as it should be remembered that there is a possibility that the objection could be challenged. Caution must be exercised in the manner of objection to a specific sub-contractor so that legislation on procurement procedures is not infringed. If a specific sub-contractor is objected to without good reason it is possible the Contractor could be involved in additional costs for which he may be entitled to reimbursement under the Contract.

Under Clause 4(4) the Contractor is fully responsible for all sub-contracted work and for the acts, defaults and neglects of any sub-contractor or his employees. The Engineer's acceptance of a sub-contractor in no way relieves the Contractor of this responsibility.

The provisions of Clause 4(5) (in respect of sub-contracting firms) and Clause 16 (in respect of individuals) give the Engineer power to require the removal from Site of sub-contractors or other persons in the circumstances described.

Clauses containing provisions that could relate to design work that may be carried out by a sub-contractor are as follows:

> Clause 4(2) requires notification of any design sub-contractor upon his appointment.

> Clause 4(5) covers the removal from the Works or their design of any sub-contractor in the circumstances described.

Clause 6(2) covers the supply of Drawings, Specifications, and other documents.

Clause 6(3) deals with the question of the copyright of Drawings, Specifications and other documents provided by the Contractor.

Clause 7(2) covers the supply of further documents if required by the Engineer.

Clause 7(6)(a) includes provisions for the submission of the Contractor's design information to the Engineer for acceptance.

Clause 7(6)(b) covers the provision of operation and maintenance manuals.

Clause 7(7) deals with the question of responsibility following approval and also makes it clear that the Engineer is responsible for the integration and co-ordination of the Contractor's design with the rest of the Works.

Clause 8(2) deals with the question of design responsibility.
(See also note against Clause 8(2)).

Clause 16 contains provisions similar to those in Clause 4(5) and covers the dismissal from the Works of individuals in the circumstances described.

Clauses 58(3) and 59 deal with design by nominated sub-contractors.

The above provisions cover the employment of sub-contractors in all normal circumstances. If an Employer wishes to exercise total control over the selection of a sub-contractor for employment by the Contractor for part of the Works this should be done by the use of the Nominated Sub-contract procedure (Clause 59) together with a Provisional Sum or Prime Cost item. Alternatively, and subject to any applicable procurement legislation, the Contract may simply specify the use of a particular supplier or sub-contractor and the Contractor would allow for this in his tendered rates and prices.

**Clause 8(2): Contractor's design responsibility**     The Contractor will not generally be responsible for the design or specification of the Permanent Works, but provision is made whereby the Contractor can be required to design part or parts of the Permanent Works. Under the provisions of Clauses 8(2) and 58(3) the Contractor can be responsible for the design or specification of Permanent Works only to the extent that the Contract expressly so provides.

If the Contractor is made responsible for the design of any part or parts of the Permanent Works, the exclusion of liability for design under Clause 20(2)(b) will, to that extent, not apply and responsibility for the design of such part or parts of the Works will be placed on the Contractor under Clause 20(1) (Care of the Works).

*Professional indemnity insurance*

Some standard Contractor's All Risks insurance policies (provided as required under Clause 21(1) for the insurance of the Works), will exclude all risks associated with the design of any part of the Permanent Works. Other such policies provide cover against loss of or damage to elements which are properly designed if they are lost or damaged as a result of the defective design of another part of the Works. Damage to parts defectively designed will not usually be covered.

If design responsibility is excluded under the Contractor's standard insurance of the Works policy the Contractor must consider whether to accept any liability resulting from a failure of design himself or whether to cover it by insurance or, if he employs a separate design engineer, whether or not he should require that design engineer to carry insurance against any loss arising as a result of a design failure.

In the absence of special arrangements (such as project insurance taken out by the Employer) cover against damage to a defectively designed part of the Works can be provided only by a professional indemnity insurance policy. Under the Contract, liability for a design failure will still lie with the Contractor but if the Employer requires the risk to be covered by insurance this requirement needs to be set out clearly in the instructions to tenderers and should state the minimum cover to be provided by the policy. The tenderers can also be asked to indicate any excess (or deductible amount) on their professional indemnity insurance policy.

Depending on the way any Contractor's design work is carried out (either by the Contractor in-house or by a separate design engineer) different situations may exist. If the Contractor has a current professional indemnity insurance policy it will normally provide cover to the Contractor up to the policy limit whether the design is carried out by the Contractor in-house or is sub-let to a reputable design engineer. Under the provisions of Clause 4(4) the Contractor remains fully responsible for all sub-contracted work.

Particular points to be noted by Engineers and Employers are as follows.

(a)     Under the second part of Clause 8(2) it is made clear that the Contractor must exercise all reasonable skill, care and diligence in his design.

(b)     Under Clause 4(2) notification has to be given to the Engineer of the name and address of any sub-contractor to whom any design work is entrusted upon appointment.

(c)     The requirement that liability for a failure of design be covered by insurance can be written into the Contract if the extent of design by the Contractor warrants this.

(d)     Professional indemnity insurance policies are annual policies which have to be renewed every year and provide cover only while they remain in force. Since the cover under such a policy applies only to claims made in that year and not to those arising from negligence in that year which gives rise to a claim in a later year, the Contractor or design sub-contractor need to establish the duration of the insurance required.

**Clause 10: Performance Security**  A Provisional Lump Sum Item should always be included in the Bills of Quantities for the provision of the Performance Security required under Clause 10(1). For a Guidance Note on the Performance Bond see Appendix 1.

**Clause 11: Provision and interpretation of information**

Employers seek certainty of expenditure on a project and to assist in this objective it is beneficial to both Employer and Contractor for all information held to be provided at tender stage. The effect of Clause 11(1) is that information obtained by or on behalf of the Employer relevant to the Works shall only be taken into account to the extent that it was made available to the Contractor before the submission of his tender. The interpretation of all such information remains the Contractor's responsibility. If the Employer fails to make available such relevant information at the proper time he cannot later argue that it ought to have been known to the Contractor. The Contractor would, however, always be expected to have obtained for himself any information that was otherwise readily available and if possible to have visited the Site (Clauses 11(2) and 11(3)).

*Clause 12: General*

*Adverse physical conditions or artificial obstructions.*

It is impossible for either of the contracting parties to foresee every circumstance that may affect the construction of the Works. It is, however, an essential feature of the ICE Conditions of Contract that the Contractor accepts full responsibility for physical conditions or artificial obstructions that could reasonably have been foreseen by an experienced contractor. It is the Contractor's obligation to construct the Works and he must therefore propose any measures to deal with the conditions or obstructions encountered, for the Engineer's consent.

The Parties rely on the Engineer's assessment of the effect of the circumstances encountered but the consequences of any unforeseeable risks have to be dealt with separately in accordance with the terms of the Contract. Such circumstances may result in extra cost and/or extra time becoming due to the Contractor.

It is clearly in the Employer's own interests to have an adequate Ground Investigation carried out before tenders are invited.

**Clause 12: Adverse physical conditions and artificial obstructions**

Clause 12(1) requires the Contractor to give written notification to the Engineer as early as is practicable of any physical condition or artificial obstruction encountered which the Contractor considers he could not have reasonably foreseen whether or not there is any intention to claim additional payment or time. Such notification must give details of any anticipated effects, the measures being taken or proposed and their estimated cost and any consequential delay and/or interference with the construction of the Works.

Notification of the intention to claim additional payment or an extension of time is still required and can be made at the same time or as soon as is reasonable thereafter (Clause 12(2)).

Following receipt of written notification, the options open to the Engineer under Clause 12(4) include requiring the Contractor to investigate any alternative measures that may be available for dealing with the situation.

**Clause 14: Programme to be furnished**

Clause 14 calls for the submission of a programme and general method statements for construction within 21 days after the award of the Contract (Clause 14(1)). Such a programme and method statements are intended as a management tool to indicate to the Engineer when specific areas of the Site and/or additional information and/or Drawings will be required by the Contractor and to enable an assessment to be made of any failure by the Contractor to maintain the required rate of progress on the Contract(Clause 46(1)). Provision is made for the Engineer to accept the Contractor's programme (Clause 14(2)) and accept the method statements (Clause 14(7)), but not for him to approve them.

After the Contractor has submitted his programme and/or method statements the Engineer has 21 days in which to accept them, reject them or request further information.

In respect of the programme the Contractor then has 21 days in which to submit a revised programme or provide the further information requested. When the Contractor submits a revised programme a further 21 day period is allowed for acceptance or rejection. If, after submission by the Contractor of a Clause 14 programme, the Engineer fails to respond within the 21 days allowed the programme is deemed to have been accepted as submitted.

The same specified restrictions do not apply in the case of method statements and methods of construction (Clause 14(6)) since it may well take longer than a pre-determined time to provide revised calculations etc. or verify that they are in accordance with the Contract.

It is always possible to include in the documentation for a Contract a programme or method statement for carrying out the whole or any part of the Works. Similarly the Contractor can be required to submit his programme or method statement with his tender. Such programmes and method statements could become contractual requirements which the Engineer may not change without the agreement of the Parties. Should any outside influence prevent compliance with any such programme or method statement the responsibility for the delay that occurred or for any additional costs arising as a result of the delay could be the responsibility of the Employer.

**Clause 19: Safety and security**

Liability for safety is imposed by the Health and Safety at Work etc. Act 1974 and other statutes. It would therefore be inappropriate and could be misleading for such liability to be spelt out in the Conditions of Contract because the parties cannot, by their Contract, alter or avoid their respective statutory responsibilities or exclude the Health and Safety Executive's powers of intervention.

If and to the extent that special safety provisions are required in connection with a specific project, such provisions can properly and appropriately be included in the Specification (which, like the Conditions of Contract, is itself a Contract document) or in the Health and Safety Plan.

*Clauses 20 to 25: General*

Attention is drawn to the fact that the liability clauses - Clause 20 in respect of the Works and Clause 22 in respect of third-party responsibilities - place full responsibility on the Contractor (save, in respect of the Works, for the Excepted Risks listed in Clause 20(2) and, in respect of third-party liabilities, for the exceptions listed in Clause 22(2)).

Clauses 21 and 23 provide safeguards for the Employer by ensuring, through the insurances that the Contractor is required to provide (up to the limits of indemnity stated in the policies), that the Contractor will be able to meet any obligations that arise and for which he is responsible under Clauses 20 and 22.

The Contractor may have a limit of indemnity on his third-party policy that is in excess of the limit stated in the Contract. This would provide the Contractor (and therefore the Employer) with additional protection because the Contractor's liability is not limited to the minimum amount stated in the Contract. However, the Contractor in all cases remains liable for the total amount should any claim be settled at an amount in excess of the minimum amount of insurance cover required under the Contract (Clauses 21(1) and 23(3)).

The Contractor's responsibility to carry employer's liability insurance is a statutory obligation and thus needs no provision in the ICE Conditions of Contract.

No reference is made to professional indemnity insurance for any design work required under the Contract. Design of Temporary Works that is incidental to work being carried out under the Contract is normally covered under the policy provided for the insurance of the Works (Clause 21). Design liability for any part of the Permanent Works, if it is to be covered by insurance, would have to be covered under a separate special professional indemnity insurance policy agreed by the Parties (see note against Clause 8(2)).

**Clause 20: Care of the Works**

Under Clause 20(1)(a) the Contractor is made fully responsible for the care of the Works and for all materials, plant and equipment for incorporation therein from the Works Commencement Date (defined in Clause 41(1)), normally until substantial completion.

Under Clause 20(1)(a) the Employer takes over full responsibility for completed work from the date of issue of a Certificate of Substantial Completion. It is therefore essential for the Engineer to give the Employer advance notice of his intention to certify completion so that any requisite insurance can be arranged.

**Clause 21(1): Insurance of the Works etc.**

The Contractor's insurance policy covering the Works must be for the full replacement cost plus an additional 10% to cover additional costs that may arise incidental to the rectification of any loss or damage, but there is no requirement under the Contract for the Contractor to insure his own plant and equipment.

The Contractor may, for his own protection, have some insurance cover for his own plant and equipment against loss through accident, fire, theft and the like.

**Clause 25(1): Evidence and terms of insurance**

It is in the Employer's interests that insurance policies taken out on his behalf are verified as meeting the requirements of the Contract and that there is evidence of payment of premiums.

**Clause 25(2): Excesses**

The excesses carried by a Contractor on his insurance policies must be disclosed at the time of tender by his entering the relevant amounts in Part 2 of the Appendix to the Form of Tender. The excesses (or uninsured losses) that the Contractor carries under his insurance policies are the Contractor's own responsibility. Although it should be verified that the excesses quoted are not too high for a particular project, it would not be appropriate for them to be queried unless they appear to be unduly large in relation to the known resources of the Contractor.

**Clause 26: Giving of notices and payment of fees**

Unless indicated otherwise in the Contract, all notices will be given by the Contractor and any fees required will be paid by the Contractor with the cost being reimbursed under Clause 26(2).

It is not intended that the Contractor should be responsible for obtaining any planning permission in respect of the Permanent Works or for any Temporary Works designed by the Engineer in their designated positions on Site.

If any planning permission as required under sub-clause (3)(c) has not been obtained prior to commencement of work on Site or in due time the warranty given ensures that the Contractor will be granted an extension of time for completion of the Works and be reimbursed for any additional costs incurred should there be any delay in the granting of the planning permission required.

**Clause 27: New Roads and Street Works Act, 1991**

The Contractor must be given full details of all conditions or limitations imposed by the highway authority or by any other responsible authority when a licence is granted or consent is given for the carrying out of street works covered by the Act. Other authorities may include but are not limited to traffic, bridge, sewer and transport authorities.

Statutory obligations arising under the New Roads and Street Works Act 1991 may extend beyond the date of issue of the Defects Correction Certificate.

**Clause 36: Quality of materials and workmanship and tests**

Quality Assurance procedures are not referred to as such in the Seventh Edition of the ICE Conditions of Contract. It should be made clear in the tender documentation if they are required and details should be given in the Specification.

**Clause 41: Works Commencement Date**

The Works Commencement Date is defined as one of three alternatives and is the starting date for the time allowed for the completion of the Contract, irrespective of when work actually commences.

**Clause 43: Time for completion**

Either the Employer or the Contractor is required to state in the Appendix to the Form of Tender the completion time for the whole of the Works or completion times for each of the separately identified Sections comprising the whole of the Works.

Where completion times are stated for separately identified Sections of the Works it is necessary to ensure that the Sections so identified plus "the Remainder of the Works" cover the whole of the Works.

**Clause 44: Extension of time for completion**

Under Clause 44(2) the Engineer must make an assessment of the delay suffered by the Contractor upon receipt of any particulars of delay under Clause 44(1). In addition, in the absence of any notification, the Engineer may make a similar assessment if he considers that the Contractor has in fact suffered a delay. In either event the Contractor must be notified in writing of the Engineer's assessment.

This requirement is included to ensure the timely recording by the Engineer of any delay suffered or claimed to have been suffered by the Contractor, but there is no need for any decision to be made at that time as to whether any extension of time for completion of the Works should be granted.

Under Clause 44(3) the Engineer has a duty to grant an interim extension of time for completion as soon as he considers that such an extension is due. This is to ensure that the Contractor does not incur additional cost by accelerating progress unnecessarily due to doubt as to whether or not an extension of time will be granted. If a claim for an extension of time is rejected the Contractor must be notified without delay.

**Clause 47: Liquidated damages for delay in substantial completion**

Clause 47 covers in detail the different situations that can exist either in dealing with the whole of the Works (Clause 47(1)) or where the Works is divided into Sections (Clause 47(2)). There is also provision for a reduction in the damages payable should any part of the Works or part of a Section of the Works be certified as complete.

When the Works is divided into Sections the Appendix to the Form of Tender states the Liquidated Damages payable should completion of any of the separately identified Sections of the Works (including the Remainder of the Works) be delayed.

It must be noted that the liquidated damages for delay quoted in the Appendix to the Form of Tender are alternatives and that if completion dates are quoted or required for Sections then liquidated damages should not be quoted for failure to complete the whole of the Works within the overall time for completion.

Provision is made in Clause 47(4)(a) for a limit to be placed on liquidated damages if this is thought to be appropriate.

Clause 47(4)(b) provides that if no sum or sums for liquidated damages are quoted in the Appendix to the Form of Tender then no damages, whether liquidated or unliquidated, will be payable.

Clause 47(6) sets out the procedure to be followed if, after liquidated damages have become payable, the Engineer issues a variation order or accepts that a Clause 12 situation or any other situation outside the control of the Contractor exists which in either event will involve further delay to that part of the Works.

In such a case the Employer's entitlement to liquidated damages is suspended until the further delay comes to an end. Both the commencement and termination of such further delay must be notified in writing by the Engineer.

**Clause 49 : Work outstanding**  It should be noted that the ICE Conditions of Contract unamended are not suitable for landscaping work or tree planting etc. for which an extended period of care and maintenance is usually required.

If a Contract let under the ICE Conditions of Contract does include an element of landscaping work or tree planting it must be made clear that any extended care and maintenance requirements that have to continue beyond the end of the Defects Correction Period will not be considered as defects to be remedied before the issue of the Defects Correction Certificate. Payment of the balance of the retention money, due to be paid under Clause 60(6), will therefore not be delayed on account of such outstanding work.

**Clauses 51(1) and 52(1): Ordered variations and their valuation**  Clause 51(1) specifically permits the ordering of variations during the Defects Correction Period. In the valuation of such variations Clause 52(1)(b) permits account to be taken for example of the fact that by then the Contractor may well have left the Site and may need to return to it specially.

Clause 52 makes it clear that all efforts should be made to agree the value of a variation and the delay consequences before the varied work is carried out.

**Clause 53: Additional Payments**  The procedure for claiming additional payments under the Contract is set out in detail in Clause 53. The Contractor's right to payment is subject to him providing details of his claim to the satisfaction of the Engineer.

**Clause 54: Non-removal of Materials and Contractor's Equipment**  It should be noted that there is no provision for goods or materials owned by the Contractor becoming, when on Site, the property of the Employer.

**Clause 59: Nominated Sub-contractors**  Whether or not Nominated Sub-contractors are to be used is a choice made by the Employer, on the advice of the Engineer. In many cases it may be possible to select the Nominated Sub-contractor during the pre-tender stage of the procurement thus allowing tenderers to take the work required fully into account.

Provision is made under Clause 59(1) for the Contractor to be able to object to the employment of a particular Nominated Sub-contractor against whom he has a reasonable objection or who declines to enter into a sub-contract containing provisions accepting obligations generally similar to those undertaken by the Contractor.

Particular note should be taken of Clause 59(1)(d) under which the Nominated Sub-contractor can be required to provide a performance security that is acceptable to the Contractor, and also of the procedure set out in Clause 59(4) that is to be followed in the event of a Nominated Sub-contractor's default.

In any case of a Nominated Sub-contractor's default the Contractor must notify the Engineer in writing before any action can be taken. The first option open to the Contractor, with the written consent of the Engineer, is to terminate the Sub-contractor's employment and to recover damages from the Sub-contractor or under the security provided by the Sub-contractor. The Engineer must then take action under Clause 59(2) and renominate or take such other action as he deems to be appropriate.

If the Engineer, because of design or other considerations, does not agree to the termination of that Nominated Sub-contractor's employment Clause 59(4)(b) provides that the Engineer must issue appropriate instructions under Clause 13.

When a sub-contractor has been nominated it should be borne in mind that the Employer may in certain circumstances have a residual responsibility if the Contractor is involved in additional costs and delays which he could not have reasonably foreseen and which may therefore entitle him to reimbursement under the Contract.

**Clause 60: Payment Provisions**

The payment provisions now take account of the requirements for the Housing Grants, Construction and Regeneration Act 1996 with respect to timing and the provision of information.

There is no change in the traditional procedures for payment against interim and final certificates.

**Clause 60(2): Monthly payments**

This Clause maintains the requirement that the final date for payment by the Employer against an Engineer's Certificate is 28 days after the date of delivery of the Contractor's monthly statement to the Engineer or the Engineer's Representative.

There is however an additional requirement whereby the Engineer has to issue and deliver his Certificate to the Employer (with a copy to the Contractor) within 25 days of the date of delivery of the Contractor's monthly statement to the Engineer's Representative.

Payment to the Contractor becomes due on certification by the Engineer with the final date for payment being within 28 days of delivery of the monthly statement to the Engineer or the Engineer's Representative.

**Clause 60(5): Retention**

The rate of retention to be deducted in accordance with Clause 60(5) is to be stated in the Appendix to the Form of Tender, Part 1 and it is recommended that this should not exceed 5% . The limit of retention has also to be stated in the Appendix to the Form of Tender, Part 1 and it is recommended that this should not exceed 3% of the Tender Total.

**Clause 60(7): Interest on overdue payments**

Clause 60(7) states that interest is due to be paid for each day a payment is overdue and that the interest is to be compounded monthly.

As the Engineer is required to certify on the basis of the statement submitted by the Contractor under Clause 60(1) the Contractor when submitting each monthly statement should include the amount of all interest that he claims as due under Clause 60(7) up to that statement date in his monthly valuation under Clause 60(1)(d).

The bank whose base lending rate is to be used for the calculation of interest must be specified in the Appendix to the Form of Tender.

Clause 60(7) makes provision for the payment of interest on sums payable to the Contractor after certificates have been corrected by an arbitrator.

**Clause 60(9): Certificates** This Clause provides that the Engineer's certificate shall also serve as the Employer's notification to the Contractor of the amount to be paid and the basis on which it was calculated. As the Engineer's certificate has to be issued at least 3 days before the final date for payment the Contractor has at least 3 days notice of the reduction made by the Engineer from the amount claimed by the Contractor in his statement.

If the information is not provided with the Engineer's certificate the Contractor is entitled to ask for full details as to how the amount certified by the Engineer has been arrived at. This information could be essential to enable the Contractor to make payments at the time they are due to any sub-contractors employed on the Contract. Details of any alterations in the rates claimed by the Contractor for new or changed items or any reduction in the quantities claimed could also be necessary so that the Contractor can decide whether to indicate his dissatisfaction with the valuation and the certificate issued under the provisions of Clause 66(2).

**Clause 60(10): Payment advice** This Clause supplements the provisions of Clause 60(9) and requires that the Contractor be notified by the Employer at least one day before a payment is due if the payment being made will differ in any respect from the amount certified by the Engineer. Details of how any amount being withheld has been calculated and the grounds for so doing have to be stated.

**Clause 64: Default of the Employer** This Clause makes provision if the Employer is in default and sets out the events upon which the Contractor may rely to terminate his employment under the Contract after giving due notice to the Employer. This Clause balances the provisions of Clause 65 which covers any default of the Contractor.

## CLAUSE 66: AVOIDANCE AND SETTLEMENT OF DISPUTES

This Clause is drafted to comply with the adjudication provisions of the Housing Grants, Construction and Regeneration Act 1996. The intention is that the adjudication procedure provided for by the Act's associated "Scheme for Construction Contracts" should not apply.

**Clause 66(1): Avoidance of disputes** The disputes procedure now includes options for both conciliation and adjudication before there is a reference to arbitration. The intention behind Clause 66 is to overcome where possible the causes of disputes and, in those cases where disputes are still likely to arise, to facilitate their clear definition and early resolution preferably by agreement. It is possible there could be consequential savings in both time and cost.

**Clause 66(2): Matters of dissatisfaction** If at any time the Employer or the Contractor is dissatisfied with any decision opinion instruction direction certificate or valuation of the Engineer or with any other matter in connection with or arising out of the Contract or the carrying out of the Works the matter has to be referred to and decided by the Engineer.

The Engineer has to give his decision on all matters included in the written submission of the referring party within one calendar month after receiving that written submission. This decision of the Engineer is an essential preliminary before the Disputes procedure set out in Clause 66 can come into force.

If either party is dissatisfied with the Engineer's decision or if a decision has not been given within the time allowed either party may serve a Notice of Dispute.

**Clause 66(3): Disputes**

This Clause sets out what can give rise to or constitute a dispute or difference leading to a Notice of Dispute.

***Settlement of disputes***
***Clause 66(5): Conciliation***
***Clause 66(6): Adjudication***
***Clause 66(9): Arbitration***

For the settlement of disputes there are options for conciliation or adjudication before there is a reference to arbitration. It is anticipated that most disputes will be dealt with as soon as possible after they arise. With the potential for the prompt settlement of many minor disputes or differences that can arise on a Contract this should lead to considerable savings in time and cost.

**Clause 66(5): Conciliation**

After service of a Notice of Dispute the dispute can be considered under the provisions of the Institution of Civil Engineers Conciliation Procedure 1994 (see Clause 66(5)) or, after Notice of Adjudication has been given (see Clause 66(6)) may be referred to an adjudicator under the terms of the Contract. These two alternatives provide routes for a speedy settlement of most disputes.

If the recommendation of a conciliator is not accepted by either party within the laid down time limit (one month) the dispute may be referred to Adjudication or direct to Arbitration. If the decision of an Adjudicator is not accepted by either party the dispute may be referred to Arbitration within the laid down time limit (three months).

**Clause 66(6): Adjudication**

The Contract incorporates by reference the ICE Adjudication Procedure 1997 (or any amendment or modification in force at the time of the Notice of Adjudication).

Following a Notice of Adjudication, 7 days are allowed for appointing the adjudicator and referring the dispute to him, whereupon he is given 28 days (or such other period as may be permitted) in which to reach his decision.

Once a decision has been reached and notified to the parties it becomes binding unless and until the dispute (not the decision) is referred to arbitration.

A failure to give effect to a decision is excluded from the arbitration agreement leaving the parties free to seek enforcement through the courts.

If a dispute on which a decision has been given is not referred to arbitration by issuing a Notice to Refer under Clause 66(9) within three months of the giving of the decision, that decision becomes final as well as binding and cannot thereafter be challenged.

**Clause 67(3): Application to Northern Ireland**

The provisions of the Housing Grants, Construction and Regeneration Act 1996 (HGCR Act 1996) have been covered by am
in these Conditions of Contract but when the Construction Contracts (Northern Ireland) Order 1997 (CC(NI) Order 1997) was published it had a different clause numbering system from that used in the HGCR Act 1996.

For ready reference the Sections of the HGCR Act 1996 are cross referenced below to the applicable Paragraphs of the CC(NI) Order 1997. It should however be noted that there are differences in the text between the Act and the Order. The HGCR Act 1996 came into force on 1 May 1998. The CC(NI) Order 1997 came into force on 1 June 1999.

| HGCR Act 1996 Section | Construction Contracts (NI) Order Paragraph |
|:---:|:---:|
| 104 | 3 |
| 105 | 4 |
| 106 | 5 |
| 107 | 6 |
| 108 | 7 |
| 109 | 8 |
| 110 | 9 |
| 111 | 10 |
| 112 | 11 |
| 113 | 12 |
| 114 | 13 and 16 |
| 115 | 14 |
| 116 | 14(c) |
| 117 | 15 |

**Clause 69(1)(b): Labour and landfill tax fluctuation**

The new Clause 69 applies also to the Finance Act 1996 (Sections 39-71 and Schedule 5) and the Landfill Tax Regulations 1996. It is made clear that only those rates of Landfill Tax chargeable under the above Act and Regulations in force at the date for return of tenders shall be deemed to have been included in the tender rates, whether or not future increases or decreases are then foreseeable. Increases or decreases after the date for return of tenders are covered in Clause 69(2).

**Clause 71: CDM Regulations 1994**

The Construction (Design and Management) Regulations apply to all construction contracts, other than:

Site surveys;

Exploration and abstraction of mineral resources and activities preparatory thereto carried out at the site of such exploration or abstraction;

Projects for which the construction phase will not last more than 30 days and which do not involve more than 500 man days of construction;

Projects for which the local authority is the enforcing authority under the Health and Safety (Enforcing Authority) Regulations 1989;

Construction (but not demolition) where not more than 5 persons are employed at any one time; or

Construction for a private client in respect of his own dwelling.

Anybody entering into a contract where the CDM Regulations apply should study the Regulations in detail. The list of exclusions above is not exhaustive.

Under these Regulations the Employer is required to appoint, as soon as practicable, a PLANNING SUPERVISOR responsible, among other things, for the preparation and monitoring of a HEALTH AND SAFETY PLAN for the contract, or for the project of which the contract is a part.

The name of the Planning Supervisor is included in Part 1 of the Appendix to the Form of Tender, and the Health and Safety Plan for the Works and the Health and Safety Files in respect of each structure included in the Works (to the extent that they have been prepared) will be available for inspection by tenderers.

Under these Regulations the Employer is also required to appoint for the project as soon as practicable a PRINCIPAL CONTRACTOR with particular responsibilities regarding safety for the project whose name (if one has been appointed by that time) is also included in Part 1 of the Appendix to the Form of Tender.

The Contractor could also be asked to act as Principal Contractor and may also be asked to act as Planning Supervisor.

On completion of the Contractor's obligations under the Contract, the Safety File becomes the property of and must be handed over to the Employer.

Where these responsibilities are not covered by separate contracts they are likely to be covered in the Specification, with appropriate items inserted in the Bill of Quantities.

**Clause 72: Special conditions**
As indicated in the section on **Contract Documents (page** 3), special conditions may be added

**Contract Price Fluctuation Clauses**
Contract Price Fluctuation Clauses are printed in the Seventh Edition and are also supplied in loose-leaf form. When one (or more) is to be incorporated in a Contract it should be included as a special Condition.

If a Contract Price Fluctuation Clause is to be included in a Contract attention is drawn to Appendix 2 of these Guidance Notes. This Appendix sets out the views of the CCSJC on what constitutes good practice when a Contract Price Fluctuation Clause is used.

# APPENDIX 1

## PERFORMANCE BOND

***General***  The Bond may be called only if the Contractor is expelled from the Site as a result of insolvency or is removed from the Site under any other of the provisions of Clause 65. If the Contractor has not been expelled from the Works, there is sufficient redress in the Contract (e.g. retention, set-off, damages etc.) to deal with other matters which might constitute a default. The Bond relates to Clause 65 for matters of expulsion and certification subsequent to that expulsion, and to the Contractor's failure to pay the Excess Sum (or any part of the Excess Sum remaining unpaid).

**Surety Bond**  The reference to Clause 66 enables the Surety, if he so wishes, to utilise the same adjudication provisions which are available to the Contractor in order to challenge the Engineer's Certificate.

Although the Surety has the right to receive copies of any notice served on the Contractor under Clause 65(1) or any certificate served under Clause 65(4) or 65(5), and to request information or to inspect the Site, this should not be considered to be a condition precedent to payment. The only condition precedent to payment by the Surety is the service on the Surety of the **certified copy** Clause 65(5) certificate. This certificate must be certified by the Engineer as a true copy and it may be an interim certificate or a final one.

By accepting this bond, the Surety undertakes, within 14 days of receiving the certified copy of a Clause 65(5) certificate, to either pay or refer the matter to adjudication. If the Surety wishes to contest the certificate or if the Employer refuses to e.g. allow the Surety's representative to inspect the Site or provide information which the Surety requests, he must seek the decision of the adjudicator in the first instance under the provisions of Clauses 66(6) to 66(8) of the Contract. The adjudicator's decision is binding unless and until the dispute is finally determined by legal proceedings, by arbitration or by agreement.

The provision in clause 1(6) of the Bond in relation to a previous adjudication between the Employer and the Contractor prevents a second adjudication taking place on the same matter. However a safeguard is incorporated to the effect that both parties must have made submissions to the adjudicator before his decision was given. This is necessary in the event that the Contractor is unable to respond to an adjudication.

The time periods have been set so that payment is not delayed unnecessarily in the event of there being no dispute. On the other hand, in the event of a dispute, the Surety has sufficient time to protect his interests. Clause 1(7) of the Bond specifies the time for payment at 7 days from the decision of the adjudicator in the event that there is no other direction.

# APPENDIX 2

## CONTRACT PRICE FLUCTUATION

**Foreword**  Three Contract Price Fluctuation Clauses are printed in the Seventh Edition of the ICE Conditions of Contract for inclusion in a Contract as special conditions when required. Loose leaf copies are also available. The Index Figures used are compiled by the Department of the Environment Transport and the Regions and published by The Stationary Office in the Monthly Bulletin of Indices "1990 Series Civil Engineering Formula Indices" and "1990 Series Structural Steelwork Formula Indices".

The CEW Clause is provided for use in connection with Works of Civil Engineering Construction, the SS Clause is provided for use on Contracts that are wholly or predominantly in respect of Structural Steelwork and the CEW/SS Clause has to be incorporated with both the CEW Clause and the SS Clause when provision is to be made for the adjustment of price fluctuation on Contracts involving both Civil Engineering Work and Structural Steelwork.

In the Guidance Notes that follow, reference to the Contract Price Fluctuations Clause (CPF Clause) is to be taken to refer to the CEW Clause or to the SS Clause or to the CEW, the SS and the CEW/SS Clauses.

**1.  Introduction**  The CPF Clause offers valuable savings in administrative effort compared with earlier variation of price clauses. These savings are achieved because the complexities arising from the effects of price variations on a contract are reduced to one simple formula. To achieve this degree of simplification many approximations and generalizations must be made: for example, the Engineer's assessment of the proportions in which different types of work contribute to the Works as a whole and the assumption that these different types of work will be performed at a steady rate throughout the period of the Contract.

It is necessary for both the Employer and the Contractor to accept that degree of approximation which is inherent in the CPF Clause. It is equally important that particular aspects of the CPF Clause should not be viewed in isolation as being likely to produce advantages or disadvantages to either the Employer or the Contractor.

Where contracts are awarded by competitive tendering any advantages or disadvantages which tenderers foresee arising from the approximations inherent in the CPF Clause will be reflected in their tenders and are unlikely to give rise to inequitable payments.

It is desirable that a uniform method of operating the CPF Clause should be established to enable tenderers to base their tenders on uniform precepts. The CCSJC is unanimous that in most contracts the methods of operating the CPF Clause set out in sections 2-4 of this Appendix are good practice and in accordance with business sense.

If, in an exceptional case, the CPF Clause is to be operated in a different manner, the proposed alternative should be described in the tender documents to enable tenderers to take its effects fully into account in the Contract.

**2.  Retention**  The CCSJC takes the view that the contractual entitlement to any payment is dependent upon Clause 60(2) and that the CPF Clause only provides for a method of calculating the fluctuation payments due as part of that payment. Payments due under the CPF Clause will be shown by the Contractor in his monthly statement in accordance with Clause 60(1)(d). Appropriate payments will be certified by the Engineer in accordance with Clause 60(2)(a) and will thus be subject to retention in accordance with Clause 60(5).

**3.**      **Dayworks and Nominated Sub-contractors**

The CCSJC considers that the words "... based on actual cost or current prices ..." in CEW Clause (2)(d)(i) apply to both Dayworks and Nominated Sub-contractors. Thus, amounts for Dayworks, or parts thereof, and Nominated Sub-contractors, where paid at actual cost or current prices, should be excluded from the Effective Value while those amounts based on rates and prices quoted at the time of tender should be included in the Effective Value.

**4.**      **Goods and materials on Site or vested in the Employer**

The amounts included in an interim certificate pursuant to Clause 60(2)(b) in respect of goods or materials on Site or vested in the Employer are normally a percentage (in no case exceeding the percentage stated in the Appendix to the Form of Tender) of the invoiced prices of the goods or materials.

When calculating the Effective Value, the above amounts, because they are based on the invoiced prices and thus items based on actual cost, should be deducted under CEW Clause (2)(d)(i) from the amount which, in the opinion of the Engineer, would otherwise be due to the Contractor under CEW Clause 2(d)(i), i.e. they do not at that stage form part of the Effective Value at that time.

In the month in which any of these goods or materials are incorporated into the Permanent Works the value of those goods or materials at tender prices (being an element in rates in the Bill of Quantities) will form part of the estimated contract value of the Permanent Works certified under Clause 60(2)(a) and thus become part of the Effective Value at that time. The Contractor will thus be paid a monthly amount in respect of the tender value of the goods or materials under Clause 60(2)(a) plus a fluctuation payment under CEW Clause (2)(d)(i) increasing or decreasing the tender value of the goods or materials in line with the increase or decrease in the value of the Works as a whole as reflected through the Price Fluctuation Factor. The percentage of the invoiced price previously paid will effectively be deducted as a previous payment on account through the operation of Clause 60(2).

**5.**      **Comment**

Attention has been directed to the case where, during a period of high inflation, goods and materials remain on Site for a considerable time, during which the Price Fluctuation Factor increases significantly. Although, as stated in section 1, particular aspects of the CPF Clause should not be viewed in isolation the CCSJC considers that this matter requires special mention. It has been suggested that in the circumstances described the Contractor would be paid an unjustifiably higher price for goods and materials than he need have been paid had the goods and materials been subject to the Price Fluctuation Factor of the month in which the goods or materials were included in an interim certificate.

However, when goods or materials are brought on to Site expediently it contributes to timely completion and for this added safeguard the Employer has paid only a percentage of the invoiced price of the goods or materials in advance of their incorporation into the Works. The longer the goods or materials remain on Site the longer is the Contractor obliged to finance that percentage of the goods or materials which has not been paid for by the Employer. The Contractor is also responsible for replacing any goods or materials stolen or spoilt while on Site. Viewed in the context of the CPF Clause the CCSJC considers that neither party receives inequitable treatment.